Gone, but Not Forgotten

History of the Ahwaga Hotel

By

Emma M. Sedore

Tioga County Historical Society
Owego, New York
2012

Dedicated to the Tioga County Historical Society
My home away from home

Contents

Illustrations

Cover/Jacket: Front: The Ahwaga House c. 1910
Back: The Ahwaga House c. 1860s

Preface

Sometimes over the years, buildings take on a life of their own. Much like people, they are viewed in various ways. Some people have fond memories of them, some not so fond; and sometimes as they age, they are viewed as eyesores and down they go. It often happens after the fact that a lot of interesting history is revealed and people are then heard saying, "too bad it had to be taken down."

As I was writing my book about Hiawatha Island, the Ahwaga Hotel, first known as the Ahwaga House, appeared over and over again in the lives of the people and events I was researching, until I realized there was much to this old place that must be told. I began to save the articles I found and if anyone even mentioned the Ahwaga Hotel, my ears would perk up. I asked many questions, sought photographs and researched every aspect that I could.

It has been years since the idea came into my mind and other projects seemed to take precedence, but I also never quit collecting information about its history. Thankfully, there are still many people around who went there, stayed there, dined there or had some connection and they were willing to chat with me about it.

When I look at photos of the hotel now, I see more than just a big building. Sometimes I think of the stories I heard or read about and try to imagine the year and what the village of Owego was like at that time. I wish it was still here; but unfortunately, as time marched on and the demands of the modern age decided its destiny, down it came, and everything in it was dispersed, from its furniture, dishes and paintings even to its windows, sidewalks and door keys.

Another thing that is mentioned in this book that could cause a bit of confusion is the Ahwaga Hall that was located next door to the Ahwaga Hotel on the west side. For years the two were literally connected and because their names were almost the same, it could make the reader wonder which was which. In later years when the Ahwaga Hall building was owned by the Hubbards, it was known as the Hubbard block and like the hotel, it too, has been torn down.

This is not just a book of facts, but anecdotes and stories that, hopefully, will capture your interest, or at least cause you to do a double-take of the historic marker on the site.

Acknowledgements

My first thank you goes to the Tioga County Historical Society for the use of their archives, which included research books, newspaper files and photographs. Great big thanks go to Elizabeth (Bibba) Spencer who patiently read every word and checked everything from commas to proper English; and to Tom McEnteer, who confirmed that my history was on target, plus his loan of photographs from his vast collection. Bob Bassett generously loaned me postcards and other memorabilia and Louise Woodburn's family and friends will smile when they see her photo with Bobby, David and her husband.

It was my pleasure and fun to listen as my friends happily reminisced about the Ahwaga. Jane Worthing recalled the night her gang of friends all gathered there when the war was over; and because Vivien DeWitt had an accident and couldn't walk, her soldier friend swooped her up in his arms and carried her into the hotel to join them.

When Vivien told me about her friend Phyllis (Ketchum) Watson, I contacted her and she told me how she met her husband on a quiet night while the juke box played. Eudora Shuler told me about the fun she and Freddie had at Cubby's "Tilly and Billy" parties and Nancy Thomas Phillips still laughs to this day about the good times she had when she entertained there.

I am also grateful to a few people, who unfortunately, are deceased since I interviewed them: Bill and Juanita Sherwood, Dan Devine, Bob Clark, Finkle Rosenberg, and Fran Clark, who spoke to me from Florida.

Gone, but Not Forgotten
History of the Ahwaga Hotel

Chapter 1

A Prime Location

The first building on the northwest corner of Front and Church Streets where the Ahwaga Hotel would eventually stand was the store and tavern built in 1795 by Capt. Luke Bates, a former sea captain. He came to Owego about 1791 and purchased the land from James McMaster. It was a two-story wooden building, painted red and had a small county store in one part, with a long porch and benches in front. A room was built on the west end where occasional social functions were held and was also used for public meetings. In fact, the first meeting for the town of Tioga (now the town of Owego) was held there on April 3, 1800 and it also served as a court house. Horse sheds were on the bank of the river across the street. The village was described by an early settler who remembered that Lake Street was nothing more than a cow path with rail fences on each side. There were no street lights and the unpaved roads turned into muck after it rained.

Bates sold the tavern in 1803 to Charles Pumpelly and George Stevens who continued to operate it as a tavern. It burned down just before suppertime in March 1829, but was immediately rebuilt into three stories, painted white and re-named the Owego Hotel. However, that burned down in the Great Fire of 1849, which leads to the beginning of the history of the Ahwaga Hotel, first known as the Ahwaga House, built in 1852.

To this day, the Great Fire was the worst one that ever happened in the Village of Owego's history. It started about three o'clock in the morning of September 27, 1849 on the south side of Front Street near the bridge and burned a total of 104 buildings between Church and Park Streets and all of Lake. It must have looked just like a war zone with the acrid stench of burned buildings filling the air and rubble and ashes strewn everywhere.

Most people must have walked around in shock wondering what to do next. The one good thing that did happen three months earlier in June of that year was when the new Erie Railroad reached Owego. It brought in the major necessities that enabled the rebuilding of the village. By the following year, a meeting was held on December 14, 1850 with James Wright, cashier of the Bank of Owego, serving as chairman and Frederick J. Fay as secretary. It was the consensus that a new hotel should be built on the corner where the first tavern stood. It made sense and the location and timing were perfect. It would attract visitors, serve elegant dinners and offer meeting rooms and more. They were sure it would be the heartbeat of the village, if not the county, and they were right.

Some of the prominent men who formed a stock company of $25,000 were Lyman P. Truman and his brothers, Orin, Francis and George; Judge Charles P. Avery, William F. Warner, LeRoy W. Kingman, Gurdon Hewitt and about three dozen more. Many of the smaller stockholders who invested were in it more to stimulate jobs and to rebuild the business section than to make a profit. In fact, after the hotel was built, many of them sold their stock at twenty-five to fifty cents on the dollar. The cost when completed, including the furniture, was approximately $35,000. Lyman Truman and sons became the owners of half the property and they sold a quarter of it to Gurdon Hewitt.

The stock company was composed of the following prominent men: Charles Pumpelly, J. L. Pinney and son, F. J. Fay, Odell Gregory, James Ely, R. Woodford and Company, G. W. Hollenback, James Wright, H. N. Hubbard, E. D. and S. S. Truman, T. I. Chatfield, T. P. Patch, Jonathan Platt, G. H. Smith, W. A. Ely, William Pumpelly, Arba Campbell, T. M. Nichols, John Carmichael, Franklin Slossen, George Bacon, F. H. Pumpelly, Isaac Lillie, J. M. Greenleaf, C. Hungerford, Lucius Truman, Newell Matson, G. J. Pumpelly, Beers and Thomas, D. C. McCollum, C. and P. Ransom, George Forsyth and Henry Camp.

When it came to naming the hotel, it was suggested to name it the Truman House after one of the largest stockholders, Lyman Truman; but Judge Charles P. Avery thought it would be more appropriate to give it an Indian name because they were the first people here, and suggested the Ahwaga House, from which "Owego" was derived. All of them agreed, including

Mr. Truman. They began digging the cellar in March 1851 and it was ready for occupancy by April 1852.

Compared to the rest of the buildings in the village, the hotel must have looked out of place. The section facing Front Street was four stories high and wrapped its way around the corner to the three-storied Church Street section. It was a huge window-filled brick edifice with a six-columned entrance supporting two large balconies in front. The original plan for the hotel was to be three stories high, but when built to that height, some of the stockholders were dissatisfied and another story was added to the Front Street portion. The dimensions of the four-story section when built were 48 x 112 feet in size and the three-story section on Church Street was 35 x 167 feet and contained 145 rooms.

The June 17, 1852 the Owego Gazette advertised the AH-WA-GA Barber Shop, expressly for the use of the Ahwaga House. Hair cuts were 12 ½ cents, Shaves were 6 ¼ cents and 12 ½ cents for shampoos. It was "Open by daylight."

In recognition of his public spirit and enterprise, Lyman P. Truman was the guest of honor at a dinner given at the hotel in the evening of July 6, 1852. Many of the prominent men and their wives who formed the stock company attended and presented him with a silver pitcher.

A sketch of the Ahwaga House as it appeared in an 1858 newspaper.
Source: Tom McEnteer collection

Transportation to and from the railroad station was provided free, while huge black, horse-drawn stagecoaches clopped-up in front bringing in dusty, tired visitors from as far away as New York City and beyond.

One of the witnesses who watched the hotel go up was a young eleven year old boy named John D. Rockefeller. Although he was born in Richford in Tioga County, N. Y., the family moved first to Moravia and then to the town of Owego in 1849 just after the fire. Growing up, his family didn't have much money, so it is easy to imagine him looking at it with awe, thinking that if he ever became wealthy enough someday he would come back and stay at the Ahwaga House, and he did many times.

The year 1852 was also when three young members of the Mohawk tribe in Canada came to Owego for the purpose of giving concerts with the proceeds to be used in educating and Christianizing the Mohawk people. SaSaNa Loft, her brother Rok-wa-ho and her sister, Ya-go-weia came in February and presented two concerts; one at the Presbyterian Church and one at the Episcopal Church. While they were here, they were guests at Judge Charles P. Avery's home, just a few doors east of the hotel. Judge Avery had an avid interest in Indian history and enjoyed visiting with them. They boarded the train in the morning, heading for their next concert in Deposit, N. Y. While the train was stopped at the station in Deposit, N. Y., Rok-wa-ho got off to purchase tickets while the two sisters waited in the last car for him. Meanwhile, an alarm was given that the engineer of a freight train at the top of a hill eight miles back had lost control and jumped off, leaving the train to speed down the hill out of control at sixty miles per hour. Thankfully, most of the passengers were in the station restaurant. SaSaNa Loft and her sister hurried to get off and Ya-go-weia, the younger sister managed to escape, but twenty-one year old SaSaNa fell back between the cars and was crushed and scalded to death. Judge Avery had her body brought back to Owego and a funeral was held at St. Paul's Church. At first, her body was taken to the Avery vault in the Presbyterian Cemetery on Temple Street with plans to take it back to Canada in the spring; but the Judge asked permission and was granted to have her remains buried in the newly opened Evergreen Cemetery high on a hill overlooking the village. Through much effort, a monument was made and erected on her grave, where it is still in the most prominent spot in the cemetery. Many people, including school children have visited her grave since then. Before Evergreen Cemetery was established, there were several small graveyards located in the village: one at the southeast corner of Main and Court streets, one at the southeast corner of Main and Lake streets and another near the southeast corner of Main and Academy streets. These locations were desirable sites for prospective businesses and the village trustees agreed to open a new and larger cemetery high on the hill off of East Avenue where most of the bodies were reinterred. In March 1852 it was officially named Evergreen.

According to the Owego Gazette, the first wedding known to have taken place at the Ahwaga House was on January 8, 1855 when the Reverend William H. Pearne married Mr. Phineas Hedges to Miss Marvett Howe, both of Barton.

On April 12, 1861 a shot was fired from a Confederate battery in Charleston Harbor and struck Fort Sumter, which was being held by a federal garrison and the Civil War began. Three days later on April 15th President Abraham Lincoln issued a call for 75,000 militia regiments and Tioga County responded immediately. Nathaniel W. Davis, a respected lawyer and former Tioga County Surrogate judge, a New York State Assemblyman and President of the village and who also served for several years as a colonel of the 53rd and 54th regiments of the New York State militia, called a meeting on April 16th at Ahwaga Hall, next door to the hotel, to ask for volunteers. On May 3rd a reception and dinner was held for the Ithaca volunteers in the dining room at the Ahwaga House accompanied by the Whitlock band. After speeches were made, the volunteers marched back to the railroad station and some never marched back.

Another wedding held at the Ahwaga House was the marriage of Henry H Howell to Cornelia C. Wheeler, of Spencer. The Reverend William H. King performed the ceremony on July 15, 1862.

The first known death occurred at the hotel on April 3, 1862 when George Bacon died at the age of 58. He was the husband of Mary Ann Pumpelly, daughter of Charles Pumpelly. Mr. Bacon was in the general mercantile business under the firm name of Pumpelly & Bacon, and later became the sole owner. Shortly after his marriage in 1829, he purchased a three acre lot on Front Street, later the site where Gurdon Pumpelly built his beautiful home in 1907, today known as The Pumpelly House Estate. Today, a short lane near there is known as Bacon Street.

Decorated for a big event, c. 1860's.
Source: Tioga County Historical Society

Perhaps, because the Civil War was raging, things seemed to have taken a turn for the worse by April 1863 for the hotel. An ad in the Owego Gazette listed an auction on April 14 at the hotel for: "One quarter's interest in the real estate of the Ahwaga House: hotel furniture, consisting of the bedding of at least 60 beds, 19 beds, mattress and feather and other property consisting of crockery and cutlery of the Ahwaga House; also chairs, settees, carpets, bedsteads & c. the whole lately invoiced at over $4,000.00." The money from the auction allowed it to remain open.

In May 1863, a large group of soldiers returned from serving in the Civil War. With the booming of cannons and the ringing of bells, the fire department met them at the station with loud cheers and escorted them to the Ahwaga House where they were feted with a sumptuous dinner. At the same time, a large ad urged "200 Men Wanted! $250 bounty for first class recruits and $175 bounty for second class recruits for Col. Tracy's 109th N. Y. Volunteers. To the two year volunteers just returned, this chance is the best that can be offered." It added, "Captain Gorman will be in Owego at the store of Truman, Stratton & Co. for the next 15 days for the purpose of receiving recruits."

Chapter 2

Expansion & Improvement

April 1865 was an historic month. On April 9th General Lee surrendered to General Grant at the Appomattox Courthouse, Virginia and the Civil War was over. People rejoiced, but not for long, because five days later on April 14th President Abraham Lincoln was shot by John Wilkes Booth in Ford's Theater, Washington, D. C. and died the next day. When the newspapers announced the assassination of President Lincoln the whole village went into mourning. Businesses and schools closed and churches, trimmed in black, held prayer meetings. Every flag flew half-mast.

Lincoln's successor, Andrew Johnson, proclaimed May 25th as a day of fasting and prayer. Partisan bitterness was put aside, except for one report that several persons in the village openly exulted over the murder of the President. The Owego Gazette reported that while a group of people were at breakfast at the Ahwaga House, one of them said he was "glad Lincoln was assassinated and hoped Grant would be the next victim!" Another agreed with him. The paper went on to say, "But these were all leading Republicans and members of "loyal" churches, and of course were not arrested. Had either one of them been a poor laboring man and a Democrat, not many minutes would have elapsed before he would have been the guest of Sheriff Upham."

Things finally settled down into routine affairs and by the time July fourth rolled around, the celebration was extra exuberant, especially because of the close of the Civil War. The streets in Owego were crowded and a huge parade formed at 11 o'clock in front of the Ahwaga House. The Owego Fire Department proudly marched with their apparatus on display and eleven veterans of the War of 1812 rode in carriages. Services were held in the park, which we know today as Courthouse Square. Speeches were made and a long poem was read by Charles A. Munger, lawyer and poet. In the evening, after dinner was served at the Ahwaga House, the people strolled back to the park for a bang-up display of fireworks.

The January 4, 1870 Owego Gazette noted that Mark Twain came to Owego and spoke at Ahwaga Hall, next door to the Ahwaga House soon after his book, *The Innocents Abroad*, was published in 1869.

A guest who came in October 1871 was none other than Phineas T. Barnum. The papers reported that several reporters met and dined with him at Ahwaga House. His first visit to Owego had been in the summer of 1849 for several days. He held his first exhibition in Concert Hall, located upstairs at the northwest corner of Front and Lake streets. He came with Tom Thumb, the miniature showman, but not many people attended. He wasn't happy and swore he would never come back to Owego again, but he did. Concert Hall was one of the buildings that burned in the great fire in 1849. The building that occupies the site today houses Riverow Bookshop.

Phineas T. Barnum 1810-1891. He swore he would never return to Owego, but he did.
Source: Tioga County Historical Society

Horace Greeley came to Owego as the honored guest speaker for the 1871 agricultural and horse fair, held at the Main Street fairgrounds. He stayed a few days with his friend John R. Chatfield at 44 Front Street. It was the house that was razed by Gurdon Pumpelly in 1907 who replaced it with the beautiful Georgian style home that is used today as a bed and breakfast. Chatfield was a prominent citizen who had been treasurer of the Tioga County Agricultural Society for many years and was a member of the state senate in 1871-72. Greeley was a newspaper editor, founder of the Liberal Republican Party, a reformer and a politician. His New York Tribune was America's most influential newspaper from the 1840s to the 1870s.

In the spring of 1873, the hotel closed for renovations and all of the old furniture and carpets were either sold at auction or taken to Pennsylvania by one of the owners, C. T. Smith. By July, Oscar Stone became the new proprietor and made major improvements. He purchased new furniture in Syracuse; which included tables, stands and bureaus for the downstairs, made of black walnut with marble tops. The furniture for the upper floors was chestnut trimmed in black walnut. Brussels and Philadelphia ingrain carpets were installed throughout. The office and reading room followed the theme of black walnut and the dining room was furnished with upholstered oak settees and had nickel-plated ware. By August the whole house was repainted and wallpapered by Chamberlain and Raymond, of Owego.

Oscar Stone had fifteen years experience in the hotel business and planned for a grand reopening in September. Invitations were sent out for Tuesday evening, September 2, 1873 and it seemed that just about everybody came. Supper was served from 9 to 12 o'clock with dancing starting around 9:30 P.M. to the music of Wright's Full Band. Committee arrangements were made by J. C. Dwelle, F. K. Hull, F. D. Philes, T. D. Gere, George S. Stratton, C. P. Starr, John G. Hollenback, George W. Woodford and C. S. Campbell. The floor committee consisted of D. M. Goodrich, D. A. Ellis, W. A. Smyth, James W. Goodrich, George Truman, Jr., Charles A. Link and S. S. Truman. The honorary committee consisted of forty of the most prominent citizens in the county, headed by Thomas C. Platt. The outside of the building was brilliantly lit, with flags flapping in the cool night breeze and about 8 o'clock the Owego Cornet Band created a festive and welcoming atmosphere by playing the latest tunes from the balcony. In the meantime, "Old

"Old" Joe DeWitt, a lovable, fun-loving and well-respected fireman and restauranteur.
Source: Tioga County Historical Society

Grand Re-opening

OF THE

Ahwaga House.

Yourself and Ladies are cordially invited to attend a

Complimentary Reception,

To be given at the Ahwaga House, Owego, N. Y.,

Tuesday Evening, September 2d, 1873,

For the benefit of the new proprietor, Mr. Oscar R. Stone.

Music by Wright's Full Band.

Supper from 9 to 12 o'clock.   *Dancing to commence at 9 o'clock.*

Formal invitation to the Grand Reopening on September 2, 1873.
Source: Robert C. Bassett collection

Honorary Committee.

Hon. Thomas C. Platt, Owego.
Hon. Lyman Truman,   "
Hon. Wheeler H. Bristol,   "
Hon. C. A. Clark,   "
Hon. H. A. Beebe,   "
Hon. John J Taylor,   "
Hon. T. I. Chatfield,   "
Hon. A. H. Miller,   "
Hon. Wm. Smyth,   "
Hon. Stephen B. Leonard,   "
Hon. John M. Parker,   "
Dr. James Wilson,   "
Frank L. Jones,   "
John B. Brush,   "
Arba Campbell,   "
Geo. W. Hollenback,   "
F. O. Cable,   "
Dr. P. S. Stearns,   "
Robert Cameron,   "
(t) N. W. Davis,   "

Hon. Jerome Thompson, Candor.
Romanta Woodford   "
Edwin A. Booth.   "
Hon. J. B Landfield, Newark Valley.
John Davidge,   "   "
Dr. C. R. Heaton   "   "
Hon. Louis P. Legg, Berkshire.
Lucien Horton,   "
Aaron Steele, Apalachin.
Col. Wm. Ransom, Tioga Centre.
Hon. W. W. Shepard, Waverly.
Howard Elmer,   "
Hon. O. H. P. Kinney,   "
W. F. Warner, Esq.,   "
Hon. J H. Deming, Richford.
C. L. Rich,   "
F. C. Coryell, Nichols.
Eben Dunham,   "
Isaac S. Stanclift, Spencer.
Col. R. C. McNeil, Campville.

Committee of Arrangements.

J. C. Dwelle,   F. K. Hull,   F. D. Philes.   T. D. Gere,   Geo. S. Stratton,
    C. P. Starr,   John G. Hollenback.   Geo. W. Woodford,
                                        C. S. Campbell.

Floor Committee.

D. M. Goodrich,   D. A. Ellis,   W. A. Smyth,   James W. Goodrich
    Geo. Truman, Jr.,   Chas. A. Link,   D. S. Truman.

List of committees for the 1873 invitation.
Source: Robert C. Bassett collection

Joe" Dewitt put on a display of fireworks up and down Front Street. Guests began to arrive well before 9 o'clock and every nook and cranny of the hotel was crowded with people.

The parlor and main hall were filled with the scent of beautiful floral arrangements contributed by a number of prominent women. Nothing was overlooked. The head chef from the Metropolitan Hotel in New York City was hired for the event and some of the farmers from around the county donated fresh vegetables, while local merchants loaned miscellaneous articles from their shops to enhance the ambience. Long tables were set up in the center hall, but could not accommodate all of the guests at one sitting. As soon as the first group was finished eating, they made their way to the dance hall to spin and whirl to a fast-paced quadrille, or to glide into a waltz. The tables were reset five times for about 750 people. Numerous guests came from out of town, including Brooklyn, Elmira, Binghamton, Philadelphia, Syracuse, Utica, Great Bend and from all parts of Tioga County. It must have been a "wing-dinger," because it lasted until five o'clock the next morning.

The August 1873 newspapers reported that George S. Leonard (son of Congressman Stephen B. Leonard) was also doing some renovating in connection with Ahwaga House. As part owner of the Ahwaga Hall next door, he made the east side of the fourth floor of Ahwaga Hall into mini apartments as an annex for hotel guests who wanted to stay for extended periods, but preferred to furnish their own rooms. A door opened into the top floor of the hotel and stairs were installed to allow the guests to enter through Ahwaga Hall and go straight up to their rooms into the hotel without going through the lobby. A woman was hired as a matron to accommodate them.

Chapter 3

The Lurid Side

The hotel was doing a steady business with a large number of out of town guests and the good reputation of their dining room was one of the reasons why. Rooms and suites were rented to "fakirs" who advertised a cure for all kinds of diseases. All that the public had to do was to attend a lecture and wind up purchasing a bottle of liquid that probably consisted of water, herbs and alcohol, with the latter being between 10-15% proof. After they drank it and got a bit tipsy, they probably felt pretty good, until it wore off and they were left with not just their original ailments, but a hangover, as well.

Independence Day in June 1874 was observed with Adams Silver Cornet Band, playing from the balcony of the hotel while a large bonfire was built on the riverbank, where Ahwaga Park is now located. Old Joe DeWitt gave a fireworks display and nearly all of the businesses on Front Street were draped with American flags. Around 9 o'clock that evening, Joe gave a much more elaborate display of fireworks for the visitors at Hiawatha Island. Even though it was cloudy with a light mist of rain on and off, the Owego steamboat ran all day, loaded with merry crowds.

In July, an article appeared criticizing the Ahwaga House owners; "They all start out with good intentions and pay their bills, but eventually get indebted over their heads to the butcher, the baker and the candlestick maker." G. V. Chapman was the last landlord and kept the house over a year. During the first year he paid his bills promptly, but since that time he has managed to get deeply in debt, and last Monday left town suddenly, leaving even the servants of the house unpaid. The business of the house will be conducted by W. P. Raymond, who owns the property and the house will be under the management of his son, W. B. Raymond." W. B. ran it successfully for five years.

When Owego celebrated the advent of America's centennial year in 1876, at 12 midnight, all the church bells started to ring simultaneously; steam whistles at the bridge shop and locomotives of the Erie and Southern Central depots screamed and hissed and clanged. 25 rounds were fired from the old "six-pounder" (cannon) which was stationed on the bank of the river opposite the Ahwaga House, spewing black smoke into the cold night air. It was a good thing the buildings on Front Street were still new, because the booming of the cannon surely must have caused them to reverberate. Adams Silver Cornet band led a torchlight parade and marched through the streets. The stores and residences were lit and draped with flags. The pandemonium lasted about a half-hour before they finally ceased, no doubt to everyone's satisfaction of knowing that such an occurrence is but once in a hundred years. There must have been some ears still ringing the next day.

Things settled once again into a normal routine with only an occasional bit of excitement, such as minor incidents with gas-lit lamps exploding, or when an inebriated guest would blow out the flame.

In January, the Tioga County Medical Society held a dinner meeting at Ahwaga House with Dr. J. B. Benton as the guest speaker. That same month a Professor Burner of London, England lectured on health and disease at Wilson Hall around the corner on Lake Street. He advertised that if it was inconvenient to attend the lecture, people were invited to see him at the professor's parlors at the Ahwaga House, probably to sell them his version of the Kilmer Brothers Swamp Root medicine.

The lurid side of the hotel's history literally tumbled down from the ceiling of an old farmhouse in 1983, when an Owego family decided to remodel their old farmhouse on the Montrose Turnpike. As the owner poked at the loose plaster in the living room ceiling, it suddenly gave way and several small books and a tapestry pillow tumbled to the floor in a dusty, mouse-nibbled heap. She looked at them and discovered they were the personal diaries from the 1870s of Lottie Richardson, a 17 year old schoolteacher. At that time the teachers often had only a few years more of education than their students. Her bedroom was just above the living room and she had hidden her secret life, along with her hopes and dreams in the small books under the floorboards. The pillow also proved to be an interesting find. Before throwing it into a pile for burning, the owner remembered that she once read that people sometimes sewed private things inside of pillows, and upon ripping the seams open, found a small leather case. It contained letters to Lottie from her boyfriend, George Ketchum, married with two children. They were the letters that she had promised him that she would destroy.

When Lottie was just seventeen in 1874, she began her teaching career in one-room schoolhouses. For additional training, she later enrolled at the Owego Academy on Court Street. While there, she boarded with a local family who had a daughter Lottie's age. They spent many evenings strolling around the village, looking into shop windows and flirting with young men. Lottie was very attractive and admitted she had no problem with finding boyfriends. She first met her "true love" (as she put it in her diary) George on one of her strolls. She wrote how he was standing in a doorway of one of the shops and as she flirtatiously passed by, he tipped his hat and bowed low in an elaborate way. Besides working as a store clerk, he was also a fiddler in a local band and would be away from home a lot. They didn't waste any time, because by the following week they went dancing together. He told her up front that he was married and had two children and a wife, but it didn't seem to faze her. She was flattered because he was ten years older than she was. While he had engagements in other towns they wrote to each other; but she addressed the envelopes to "Georgia" as if she were writing to a girl friend. He warned her to destroy his letters and she agreed, but instead, she put them in a leather case and sewed them inside of a pillow and kept it under the floorboards of her bedroom.

It wasn't long before they had clandestine meetings in room 95 of the Ahwaga House. It would seem that they would be found out because they were well-known in the village; but, Ahwaga Hall, the building attached to the Ahwaga House, had a separate entrance with stairs going to the top floor to apartments, with an entrance into the hotel from there that George S. Leonard had constructed about a year earlier. That is probably how Lottie got around without being found out. She entered through Ahwaga Hall and he would enter the hotel through the front door and they would meet upstairs without anyone seeing them.

The last time they met there was in July 1878. Soon afterwards she discovered the inevitable: she was pregnant. He told her she had to get an abortion and took her to a woman in the town of Tioga to perform the operation.

After it was done she seemed to be feeling better; however, things took a turn for the worse and ten days later, the abortionist called a doctor, but it was too late. Lottie died at the age of twenty-one.

The newspapers printed the story, entitled, "A Sad Tale." George was arrested, but protested, pleading innocence by saying that he was just doing a young girl a favor by taking her there at her request. He was sentenced to ten years of hard labor in Auburn State Prison; but in an AP dispatch in a January 4, 1883 newspaper, it reported," Mr. George Ketchum had his sentence commuted to four years by Governor Cornell last Friday. He will be discharged February 20, 1883." The abortionist, Sarah Stalker, aged 54, was sentenced to the Onondaga County Penitentiary also for a term of ten years, but there was no news of her sentence being commuted.

Chapter 4

Re-openings & Reunions

A grand re-opening party was held on April 30, 1879 in honor of the new proprietor, the Hon. Burr J. Davis, and of course, elaborate arrangements were made. Many assistants were hired to accommodate the guests and all was in place, except for one unexpected thing: Davis became ill and couldn't leave his room! But, the party went on anyway, with out-of-town guests arriving in the afternoon. The Lyman Truman steamboat returned from Binghamton about 5:30 P.M. with nearly 300 passengers, including the City Guard Band. Many of them dined at the Ahwaga House and stayed on to enjoy the party. By 9 o'clock, large crowds filled the parlors, dining room and the halls. Afterwards, they scurried next door to Ahwaga Hall and danced to the music of White and Beman's Orchestra, of Binghamton. The floor of the hall was covered with a white canvas and the air was filled with the fragrance of flowers from the Hamlin Jones Greenhouse, in Owego. The wall was decorated with paintings and the United States flag. Between fifty to seventy-five couples continued to dance until after 3:00 A.M. For those who worked up an appetite from dancing, a second supper was served at midnight at the hotel and from the guest's comments, it couldn't have been better.

August was also a busy month. General Isaac Catlin held a reception for the first annual reunion of the 109th Civil War Volunteers at the hotel, but the actual reunion was held on Hiawatha Island on September 29, 1879. The Lyman Truman steamboat was jammed with people and by the end of the day it was reported that between 1500 and 2000 people visited the island to pay their respects.

On October 16th, guests included T. J. Cummings of the *New York Herald* and G. W. Bungay of the *New York Tribune*. Bungay was an interesting and talented man with several careers. He was a British born American poet,

You are requested to be present at a

RECEPTION

to be given the

Hon B. J. Davis,

by the citizens of Owego on the occasion of

the formal opening of the

Ahwaga House,

Wednesday Evening, April 30th 1879

Overture 9 P. M.

TICKETS. $2.00 EACH, ADMITTING GENTLEMAN AND LADY,
INCLUDING SUPPER.

WM. SMYTH & SON, PRINTERS.

Invitation to another formal opening on April 30, 1879.
Source: Tioga County Historical Society

HONORARY COMMITTEE.

HON . T . C . PLATT .	OWEGO .	HON . J . J . TAYLOR .
ORIN TRUMAN .		HON . A . H . MILLER .
J . N . DEXTER .	WAVERLY .	DR . W . E . JOHNSON .
E . O . BEERS .	ELMIRA .	HENRY CAMPBELL .
TRACY ROGERS .	BINGHAMTON .	H . E . ALLEN .
S . F . SMITH .	UNION .	CHAS . WOUGHTER .
S . B . DAVIDGE .	NEWARK VALLEY .	O . DIMMICK .
LUCIEN HORTON .	BERKSHIRE .	F . H . PAYNE .
DR . GEORGE P . CADY .	NICHOLS .	E . DUNHAM .
EPENETUS HOWE .	SPEEDSVILLE .	W . S . LAWRENCE .
CHAS . A . CLARK .	RICHFORD .	W . H . THELEMAN .
CAPT . C . F . BARRAGER .	CANDOR .	N . J . THOMPSON .
AARON STEELE .	APALACHIN .	GEO . L . CATLIN .
R . SPENDLEY .	TIOGA .	J . R . WILLMOT .
M . B FERRIS .	SPENCER .	CHAS . E . BUTTS .

INVITATION COMMITTEE.

D . M . GOODRICH .	J . B . STANBROUGH .
C . H . HYDE .	J . C . DWELLE .
F . N . MABEE .	F . D . PHILES .
G . TRUMAN, JR .	H . I . ROSS .

W . A . SMYTH .

List of committees for the 1879 invitation.
Source: Tioga County Historical Society

lyricist, journalist and abolitionist. Included in his career as a lyricist he wrote for Stephen Collins Foster and John Howard Payne, who wrote Home Sweet Home. As a journalist, he joined the editorial staff of Horace Greeley's New York Tribune, the best known and most influential newspaper of that day. He had quite a reputation as a reform writer and worked with many famous writers.

In October 1880, U. S. Senator Roscoe Conkling (1829-1888) came to Owego for a speaking engagement and stayed at the hotel. He was the leader of the movement for the nomination of Ulysses S. Grant for a third term for the presidency and probably came to encourage votes to get him re-elected. Arrangements were made for him to speak in a barn on Chestnut Street and the newspaper noted that he was less than pleased.

Grover Cleveland visited the Ahwaga, but it was while he was mayor of Buffalo in 1882. His rise in politics was amazing. Elected mayor in 1882, he was then elected Governor of New York State by 1883 and by 1885 he was President of the United States. They sure don't do things like that today.

In May of 1882, as a new sewer line was being installed from the hotel to the river, passing under one of the stores on the south side of Front Street, some of the timbers from the old Ithaca and Owego railroad (1834-1849) were found about a foot below the pavement in good shape.

By August of 1883, B. J. Davis made some important improvements in the hotel. He moved the barroom down to the basement and hired R. D. Willard to manage it. Two billiard tables were also placed in the new location. The old barroom was converted to a sales room for visiting salesmen.

Another very good decision Davis made in 1883 was to hire Catherine (Kate) Roach as a waitress; it worked out well because she was employed there for forty years. She turned out to be credited for the excellent reputation of the Ahwaga, always making the guests feel at home and always making sure they had enough to eat.

In 1886, Davis added a one-horse omnibus to his stables to transport guests to and from the railroad stations. By December 1889, he sold it and had it shipped to the new owners in Hornellsville. He was always making the hotel more comfortable and accommodating for the guests. He installed a public pay phone in 1891, the same year Secretary of the Navy Benjamin F. Tracy was registered there.

Senator Roscoe Conkling 1829-1888. At the Ahwaga October, 1880 for a speaking engagement in Owego.

Grover Cleveland 1837-1908. At the Ahwaga while Mayor of Buffalo. Elected as 22nd and 24th President of the U.S.

In the spring of 1892, Davis continued to update his hotel by having the dining room refurbished. The walls and ceiling were decorated with a long mirror hung horizontally on the north wall. The small, round tables were replaced by a more modern style, being rectangular and made of antique oak, with handsome high back chairs to match. In the fall, he installed new wash bowls and slabs of dark Tennessee marble, furnished by the Donley Brothers, of Binghamton.

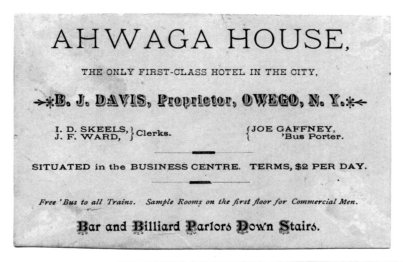

1892 business card with a whimsical drawing on the reverse side.
Source: Robert C. Bassett collection

In June of that year, the hotel had its most famous guest, John D. Rockefeller, who registered with his family, including his brother William. They probably remembered seeing the hotel being built when they were just boys on their way to school at the old Owego Academy on Court Street.

The first Jewish wedding in Owego occurred on August 18, 1895 when Samuel Matshak was married at Ahwaga Hall. Matshak came to Owego the year before and worked for his cousin, Robert Tuck, as a cutter in his leather coat factory. Twenty years before, George Tuck operated a clothing store at the west end of the Ahwaga House. By 1907, Matshak was a rich wholesale dry goods merchant in New York City; but for some reason, he committed suicide at the age of 39.

Burr J. Davis died in May 1897. His son-in-law John F. Ward assumed management of the hotel and in 1909 officially purchased it from Davis' heirs. He catered to the many traveling salesmen who stayed there on brief visits and it paid off. He also spent thousands of dollars making improvements such as installing large plate glass windows in the south and east walls of the reading room, facing Front and Church Streets, and bathrooms connected to the sewer line on Church Street, in all of the hotel rooms.

Waitress Kate Roach recalled how, in 1902, just before closing, a thin older man came in with a woman and three girls. They looked tired and hungry and sat down in the dining room. She thought they were theater people. She waited on them and they ate heartily and when they finished, the man said, "we are going to stay here three days and we want you to wait on us." She soon learned that it was John D. Rockefeller. He even made a point of stopping at the desk before going to their rooms to tell the proprietor, "We'll want that same waitress. We came in late tonight and in any other hotel the waitress would have worn a long face and given us the nearest thing that came in hand. There was a smile on this girl's face from ear to ear and I never was forced to eat so much in all my life."

In the fall of 1904, one of the guests was Thomas F. Goodrich, married to Elizabeth Ransom, originally from the town of Tioga. He was an insurance executive in Brooklyn and had just retired to make his home in Owego. His wife owned Hiawatha Island and they planned to use it as their summer home. He was staying at the hotel to vote, planning to return to Brooklyn to wrap up the sale of his business when he was stricken with a heart attack and died November 15. He was a close friend of Charles D. Marvin, who later became the mayor of Owego. Several years after Goodrich died, Marvin married Goodrich's widow.

One of the biggest events that ever took place at the hotel and the largest number of the most notable people ever gathered before or since at one time was on Tuesday, November 15, 1904 in celebration of the triumphant election of Theodore Roosevelt and Charles W. Fairbanks. It was a buckwheat pancake breakfast hosted by United States Senator and Mrs. Thomas Collier Platt which was attended by one hundred sixty-eight guests. Included among the guests were prominent Republican political leaders in the state and federal governments, such as Senator Chauncey Depew, Lieutenant Governor Woodruff, Congressman-Elect J. Sloat Fassett, Congressman Sereno E. Payne, Republican leader of the House of Representatives, Assistant Treasurer of the United States, Hamilton Fish, the Honorable Lemuel Ely Quigg, the Honorable Job E. Hedges of New York and Attorney General-Elect Julius Mayer and officials from every part of the state and all

Chauncey DePew 1834-1928. New York Senator who attended Tom Platt's famous pancake breakfast at the Ahwaga in 1904. Source: Tioga County Historical Society

of Tioga and Broome Counties. A few of the dignitaries were hosted in the private homes of L. H. Leonard, Frank M. Baker, William A. Smyth and Charles E. Parker.

Senator and Mrs. Platt arrived by a special Erie train with a large group of invited guests and were driven directly to the Ahwaga Hotel. The entire hotel was reserved for them, and they continued to arrive on every train during the night and the following morning. A mammoth pie was made and delivered the night before. It was ten feet long, three feet wide, two inches deep and weighed over two hundred pounds. The words, "The Kind Our Mother Made" were written on top. It was donated by the Republicans of Waverly and presented to Senator Platt and his wife; in fact, the pie tin was shipped to Mrs. Platt afterwards as a souvenir.

To say the hotel was elaborately decorated is an understatement. There were American flags of all sizes everywhere. The large dining room where breakfast was served was artistically transformed. The side walls were adorned with sheaves of wheat and ears of corn and lighted Jack-o-Lanterns

Thomas Collier Platt 1833-1910. The Ahwaga Hotel was his official voting address.
Source: Tioga County Historical Society

were placed in the corners. Large pictures of Roosevelt, Fairbanks and Platt, surrounded by flags, were prominently displayed. The table decorations followed the fall theme of pumpkins, crookneck squash and corn. Suspended from the ceiling over Senator Platt's seat was a huge eagle with outspread wings. When waves of air moved it, it appeared to be floating. The guests were seated at four tables which extended the entire length of the room and identified as tables A, B, C and D. Speeches were made by nine speakers and telegrams and letters of regret were read from those who were unable to come. The speeches were met with great enthusiasm. When a well-received point was made, the guests grabbed their napkins and waved them with a hearty yell that probably rattled the rafters. All of this took place from 11 A.M. to 2:30 P.M. It probably took them that long to eat, because the menu consisted of tomato pickles, baked beans, baked apples with cream, venison steak, hot biscuits, creamed potatoes, buckwheat cakes, sausage, maple syrup, cider, crullers, ginger cookies, mince, apple and the gigantic 200 pound pumpkin pie and tea and coffee. Most of the pie was later donated to the residents of the county poorhouse. It makes you wonder if that is how "doggie bags" got their start. Perhaps it explains why two years later, five new bathrooms were installed.

The Thomas C. Platt funeral at the Presbyterian Church, March 9, 1910.
Source: Tioga County Historical Society

In 1906 the hotel was still going strong, attracting a lot of guests and others who just came to dine. The hotel was known for great food and drink. One of their ads read, "It is intended for those who appreciate quality; for those gentlemen who enjoy a thoroughly matured rich old Kentucky liquor. I. W. Harper whiskey sold by the Ahwaga Hotel, Owego, N. Y."

On August 30, 1907 another death occurred at the hotel. Sixty-nine year old Frederick Hewitt died while visiting his former fiancée, Sarah Peck, daughter of the deceased Owego Baptist clergyman, Philetus B. Peck. They never married because his brother, Gurdon Hewitt broke up their plans many years earlier, but it seemed that they never stopped caring about each other.

In June, Thomas C. Platt's sons and wives, Mr. and Mrs. Henry B. and Mr. and Mrs. Frank Platt, drove to Owego to spend a weekend at the Ahwaga where they gave a dinner party. The following month, Mrs. Henry B. (Grace) Platt came back to Owego in a coffin. The Erie Railroad car that carried her body was elaborately decorated with laurel. She died of Typhoid fever on July 14, 1907 and was buried July 17 in the family plot in Evergreen Cemetery. It was just seven months after Frank's daughter, seventeen year-old Ellen B. Platt died of the same disease and was also buried in Evergreen.

The Platt funeral at Evergreen Cemetery; preparing to remove the casket for burial.
Source: Tioga County Historical Society

Lowering the casket of Thomas C. Platt into the grave at Evergreen Cemetery.
Source: Tioga County Historical Society

In 1909, Owego held its Old Home Week from August 1 through the 5th and throngs of people crowded the streets every day. The hotel must have been filled with guests, keeping the staff on their toes. Hattie Williams was the pastry chef and her pies, cakes, cookies and other delights sated everyone who ate them.

Probably because Owego's Old Home Week was planned for August, Mr. Ward installed large plate glass windows in the front and east sides of the sitting room, giving it a more up-to-date look and making it a much brighter place.

During 1909s Old Home Week there wasn't a dull moment in the village, including at the Ahwaga House where visitors were registered from all over the country. Flags were draped from many of the residences and all of the businesses. Strings of lighted Japanese lanterns were hung on porches and light bulbs were hung everywhere, much like our Christmas lights are today. A large parade was held on August 5th consisting of bands, elaborate floats and groups from just about every organization in and out of town.

Judging was done from the balcony of the Ahwaga and newspapers reported every detail. The following year, a new concrete sidewalk was laid on the Church Street side of the hotel.

Senator Platt, whose health had been rapidly failing, passed away on March 6, 1910. His body lay in state in the chancel of the First Presbyterian Church on North Avenue, where thousands of people filed past. Floral tributes arrived from President and Mrs. Taft, the New York State Legislature, the Republican State Committee, Wells Fargo Express Company, and the New York State delegation in Congress. All of the schools and businesses were closed during the funeral. Many dignitaries came to Owego for this solemn occasion, with several staying at the Ahwaga, his official voting address. He only had to walk across the street to Defiance Fire Company No. 5 to cast his ballot; but by 1907 he was so ill that had to be carried across the street to vote.

The Ahwaga had a very important visitor on October 24, 1910 when Teddy Roosevelt came to town. He gave a speech to a large crowd from the balcony to make a personal appeal to Tioga County voters to support the Republican ticket. He had just finished his term as president and preferred to be called Col. Roosevelt. The Owego band played before he arrived and General Catlin came to hear him while students climbed on the rooftops across the street to get a better view. Roosevelt also recognized J. Alden "Tod" Loring, the naturalist of Owego, who had accompanied him on his safari to Africa for a year in 1909 and had just recently returned. The newspaper reported that as he was waiting in his car in the midst of the crowd, he saw Loring's mother and sister waiting in another car.

Teddy Roosevelt,
26th President of the United States

In a cheerful manner, he stood up, waving his hat to Mrs. Loring, shouting, "Mrs. Loring, I am pleased to meet you. I swear by J. Alden Loring!" She smiled and nodded her head to him as he sat back down.

Teddy Roosevelt speaking from the Ahwaga hotel balcony, October 24, 1910.
Source: Tioga County Historical Society.

Alternate view of Teddy Roosevelt speaking on October 24, 1910.
Source: Tioga County Historical Society

Unidentified men posing in front of the Ahwaga hotel, c. 1910.
Source: Tioga County Historical Society

Chapter 5

The Heat's On

It was not unusual for residents who lived outside of the village to reside at the Ahwaga for the winter. One of them was Brigadier-General Isaac S. Catlin who had an estate on Marshland Road. The newspaper noted that he had returned to his farm in May of 1914. He was General Benjamin F. Tracy's brother-in-law and fought in the Civil War where he lost his leg by an explosion of a mine while leading a charge at Petersburg, Virginia. After the war he was elected the District Attorney of Tioga County from 1865 to 1868 and then went on to practice law in Brooklyn and was later elected twice as the district attorney of Kings County, in Brooklyn.

The women's suffrage leaders got off to an early start on February 10, 1915 by holding their Victory 1915 campaign meeting at the Ahwaga House, just three years before women had the right to vote. Of the ninety-four women in the village of Owego who voted for the first time, the first was Harriet L. Moe, of McMaster Street on January 1, 1918.

An event that drew crowds from March 13 through the 20th in 1915 was Owego's first auto show. Several cars featured were the Chandler for $1,295, the Paige-Detroit for $1,075 and Oldsmobile's for $1,285 for the four cylinder and $2,975 for the six cylinder. Cars were lined up outside with their prices boldly printed on posters. There was even a special invitation for ladies to inspect them. Three of the cars were parked inside in what was referred to as the sample room where the large windows allowed passers-by to look in and check them out. One was even parked in the reading room. The distinguishing features of the Paige "36" bodies were roominess, beauty and comfort. The bodies were made of pressed steel. Other cars featured seats for five people and upholstery in genuine leather over curled hair, making the cushions over-stuffed and comfortable. The Chandler six got sixteen miles to the gallon. The show drew a lot of attention. Five years later, another automobile show was held at the Ahwaga and by the end of the 1920s seventy-five percent of households in America owned a car. Driver's licenses were not required until June 1925, so anyone who bought one would just ask the salesman how it worked, climb in and drive it home. If they were lucky, they arrived safely. The newspapers were full of accident reports: fender-benders, running into trees, knocking people down. Unfortunately, many of them ended with tragic results.

It was always big news when John D. Rockefeller came to town and his trip on Tuesday afternoon, June 17, 1919 was no different; this time his group came in a large Simplex and two Pierce-Arrow cars with another car following with the baggage. The party consisted of John D., William and his wife, relatives, secretaries and extra chauffeurs, fourteen, total. Although they booked rooms at the Arlington Hotel in Binghamton, they came to Owego and ate lunch and dinner at the Ahwaga. They also visited their old friends and their old homestead across from Hiawatha Island. They looked forward to having their favorite waitress, Kate Roach, serve them their meals. She told the reporters, "They've been coming here, old and young and little and big for the last thirty-five years." "Mr. John D. and Mr. William are very smart men and they are very nice to plain people. Mr. John D. told me that he never had such a nice trip before in his life as the one he had here. And Mr. William said the same thing. And, more than that, this time they all stayed overnight at the Arlington in Binghamton with fourteen rooms for fourteen people, and when Mr. John D. was leaving he said to me that he had such a good time that the next time he comes, and that will be next year, he is going to stay overnight here at the Ahwaga with all of his party. He certainly knows a good hotel when he sees it. And more than that, she added, he said that he never tasted better custard pie than I served him today."

When America entered World War I in April 1917, the first Tioga County contingent left September 6 for Fort Dix. It consisted of only eight Owego men. One of them was John Sittelotta, age twenty-four. He came from Italy just six years before and unfortunately, also had the distinction of being the first soldier from Tioga County who was killed the following May. Before they left, a crowd of about eight hundred people saw them to the train. An

*After a huge welcome home parade in September, 1919
all of the WWI vets were presented with the above medal.
Source: Thomas McEnteer collection*

elaborate dinner was served to them at the Ahwaga House where host, John Ward, presented each man a box of cigars. As the train pulled out the Boy Scout band played *Tipperary*. The second contingent of sixty-two men left two weeks later after staying overnight at the Ahwaga. Compared to the send-off of the first contingent, this one was twice as large. A parade was held and people came from all over the county. All of the businesses in Owego, Newark Valley, Candor and Spencer were closed from 11:00 A.M. to 3:00 P.M. The female employees of the Kayser Glove factory gave each man a box lunch wrapped in white paper, tied in red, white and blue ribbons. It contained two ham sandwiches, a half-pound of candy, an orange, a boiled egg, fig newtons and Nabisco wafers. A telegram of thanks was received later from "62 grateful boys." The Ahwaga House did its patriotic duty every time a contingent left. Thankfully, by November 1918 the Germans surrendered. In September 1919 elaborate ceremonies were held for the returning World War I veterans. Medals were presented to every soldier, sailor and marine who served in the war, and of course, a rousing parade marched through the streets.

In October 1920 Governor Alfred E. Smith came to the hotel while running for re-election. His opponent was Nathan L. Miller who defeated him

Alfred E. Smith 1873-1944 the 42nd Governor of New York State. At the Ahwaga, 1920.

by 75,000 votes. However, Smith was again elected in 1922, 1924 and 1926, making him, at that time, one of the three New York State governors to be elected for four terms.

August 1921 was an eventful month for Dwight D. Decker. After managing the Ahwaga for a couple of years, John F. Ward sold it to him. Ward had purchased it from the heirs of B. J. Davis in 1909, and decided it was time to let it go. On the 28th of the month, Decker married Lucille Baldwin, better known as "Cubby," who was a great asset to him.

They made the hotel their residence and continued to keep its good reputation intact. The following year Decker purchased Hiawatha Island to use as a farm and the site for a dairy plant to supply most of the food needed for the guests. The hotel was known for the delicious meals and large por-

Dwight and Cubby Decker, owners of the hotel and Hiawatha Island.
Source: Jeanette Baldwin

1944 Aerial photo of Hiawatha Island showing the farm.
Source: Tioga County Soil and Water District

tions served; so by using the island to grow the vegetables, fruit, wheat and to process milk, Dwight saved the expense of purchasing all of it elsewhere. One of the business ads listed a five course dinner for seventy-five cents. A large wooden ferry and rowboats were used for transportation over the river. Cubby spent a lot of time at the island picking everything from tomatoes to peaches and canning them. She would often be seen driving a small pick-up truck filled with happy young kids in the back, known as the "truck gang," on their way to the island. They helped pick fruit and vegetables along with just having fun. Pigs, chickens, turkeys, sheep, goats and horses were also raised there. Some of the animals were butchered and dressed on the island. If they were expecting a large crowd at the hotel, sometimes as many as three hundred chickens were killed to serve for the event. Of course, to assist with all this work, caretakers were hired. A man named Toby Oaks was hired to bring the fresh vegetables and meat from Hiawatha Island to the hotel every day and return the next day with the garbage, which would then be fed to the animals, or composted, or thrown in the river. The caretakers often found dishes and silverware mixed in with the garbage, and after cleaning them off,

Ahwaga Hall set up for dancing, c. 1920.
Source: Tioga County Historical Society

Ahwaga Hall with a banquet in progress, c. 1920.
Source: Tioga County Historical Society

Professor Praeger's dancing class in Ahwaga Hall, November 13, 1917.
Source: Tioga County Historical Society

Church St. view showing part of Ahwaga Hotel parking garage. Note the Baptist church
in right background. Large building in the left background was the glove factory, c. 1912.
Source: David Geller collection

used them for their own families. Toby was paid ten dollars a week, plus room and board at the Ahwaga.

In October, a long time resident of the hotel, Frank D. Philes died at his apartment at the Ahwaga. His friends remembered him as Captain Frank D. Philes, the pilot for the Glenmary and Marshland steamboats in the 1880s that took visitors to and from Hiawatha Island. He was also a ticket agent for the Erie Railroad for many years.

Two years later, in 1923, the Ahwaga Hotels Incorporation was formed, merging the Owego Hotel at the southeast corner of Main and Lake Streets and the Ahwaga Hotel. Dwight's father, Dr. George M. Decker was named president and Dwight was named the managing director of the hotel corporation.

Timothy B. Oakley had been a prominent lawyer in Owego for many years and had his law office across the street from the hotel, at 214 Front. On February 28, 1924, in honor of his eightieth birthday, members of the Tioga County Bar Association held a banquet in the private dining room of the Ahwaga Hotel. The association president, Judge John M. Parker presided over the thirty members and guests who were in attendance. The room was gaily decorated with yellow paper roses and candles, and of course, there was a large birthday cake with the number "80" written on it in pink icing. Mr. Oakley was delighted and humorously reminisced about his life as a young man rafting lumber down the river to ports in Pennsylvania. He passed away in 1935 at the age of 91.

1927 was the centennial year for the incorporation of the Village of Owego. Included in the celebration was the dedication of the Ahwaga and Draper parks. However, one of the highlights was when Major Clarence D. Chamberlain, the pilot who flew from New York to Germany flew to Owego to meet John D. Rockefeller at the Ahwaga Hotel. Chamberlain just happened to be in Binghamton at the same time and John G. McPhee, secretary of the Owego Chamber of Commerce, set up the meeting. Chamberlain was accompanied by two other planes as they landed in the old A. V. Draper flying field in the town of Tioga, close to where the Shangri-La Raceway used to be. Arthur B. Stiles, chairman of the celebration, drove them into the village. After Chamberlain and Rockefeller were introduced, they crossed the street to Ahwaga Park for the unveiling of the boulder.

August 9, 1927. John D. Rockefeller is shown with Major Clarence D. Chamberlain, left and Arthur Stiles in center. The man in the rear is an aide to Rockefeller. Major Chamberlain was the first man to fly nonstop to Europe (before Charles Lindbergh, but not alone in the plane). Source: Tioga County Historical Society

They were followed by a huge crowd, where movies were filmed of them using Mr. Rockefeller's camera and Leslie Fancher's camera. Fancher was a well known Owego photographer. After Mr. Chamberlain left, he circled over the hotel, banking his wings twice in a salute. The word, "Owego" and an arrow pointing to the north had been painted in large white letters across the roof by McPhee and Eugene Leahy the day before. They were informed later that the pilots could see it clearly from 2500 feet. A huge parade was held in the evening and Mr. Rockefeller and his party of eight viewed it from the hotel balcony.

In 1928, the Owego Rotary Club met in the private dining room at the hotel, then moved to the main dining room with a curtain between them and the customers, but found it unsatisfactory. By the next summer they moved their meetings to the Owego Country Club in the town of Tioga, but by fall, were meeting at the hotel again. In January 1932, Norman Vincent Peale came to the Ahwaga as their guest speaker. The subject of his talk was, "The Pioneers of America." The following week, Major Robert Treman of Ithaca

Norman Vincent Peale 1898-1993.
Guest of the Owego Rotary Club at the Ahwaga Hotel, 1932.

spoke on hunting in the Canadian Rockies, illustrated with movies. By June 1932 they finally moved to the private room at the Green Lantern Inn on North Avenue.

The month of August 1930 proved to be a costly one for the management of the Ahwaga. A fire was discovered on the fourth floor about six o'clock on August 11th in the evening and tons of water used to extinguish it poured down to the other floors. It was later estimated that at least five hundred tons of water was poured into the attic with about two inches covering the rug in the lobby. The firemen didn't have far to travel, because the Defiance Number 5 fire department was located directly across the street where the John Barleycorn restaurant is today. They climbed the roof of the three story section of the hotel on the Church Street side to reach the northeast corner where the fire was. The probable cause was a short circuit and the amount of insurance carried on the building and its contents was about $17,000 which just about covered the loss. Water and dense smoke also entered the store of jeweler, George A. Durussel, located one door west of the lobby. There were only about fifteen guests at the time. The hotel reopened the next day, but nearly all of the rooms and halls in the main section had to be repainted and repapered, plus a large amount of plastering was required. Dwight Decker was at Hiawatha Island at the time and didn't know about the fire until he drove up and saw the commotion. Cubby was there at the time and called the fire department. It proved to be the entertainment for the night for about a thousand spectators.

Because of the fire, the hotel was almost completely refurbished and re-decorated from the walls and ceilings to new furniture and rugs. The stores and shops that occupied the street level were a radio store, a law office, a jewelry store and the office for the chief engineer of the Owego Fire Department. They also had to be cleaned and repaired. It cost thousands of dollars and almost six months to complete. The work was almost done when another huge disastrous fire struck around midnight on February 27, 1931. This one was much worse with damage estimated at $50,000.

Oddly enough, it started in the same area that the first one did, on the top northeast corner, in the attic. A guest who occupied the southeast corner room of the fourth floor heard a muffled explosion and found flames shooting from the last room at the corner. He ran downstairs to the lobby

The Ahwaga Hotel dining room, plain and simple, c. 1920.
Source: Tioga County Historical Society

and notified the fire department. The flames spread quickly into the narrow attic between the ceiling and the roof and ran along the rafters. The previous year, the flames were confined to the northeast corner, but this time they spread all the way to the western end on the Front Street side. The firemen on the roof battled the intense heat and flames while the fifty-five guests hurriedly gathered their belongings and moved into the Owego Hotel at the corner of Lake and Main. A strong odor of gasoline or kerosene was noticed by the firefighters, causing them to believe it was caused by an arsonist, but after the questioning of the guests, the staff and a number of other people by the police, nothing could be immediately proven until a couple of months later. Meanwhile, an inventory of the damage this time resulted in finding that the blaze started in room 95 on the third floor and water damage was caused to the room below and the dining room on the first floor. The walls of the adjoining rooms were badly scorched and the newly installed velvet rug in the corridor of the third floor had to be replaced. The smoke damaged the walls and ceilings on the other floors and they all had to be repapered and painted. Just about everything had to be refurbished all over again. A number of citizens volunteered to help the firemen remove furniture and personal effects, and later it was discovered that a quantity of articles were missing and never found. The poor old Ahwaga had seen better days, that's for sure.

By May, Corporal Henry J. Mitter of the State Police and Chief of Police Earl Sibley brought a suspect to headquarters for questioning. His name was Fred G. Hickein, age 33, an Owego carpenter who had roomed on the fourth floor for quite a while. In fact, he was hired to repair some of the damage following the first fire. After grilling him at length, he finally confessed. He stated that he returned to the hotel about 8:45 P.M. and went directly to his room at the head of the stairs on the fourth floor. He undressed and got into bed where he read the paper and some magazines. At 11:45 P.M. he admitted that he got out of bed, dressed and got a gallon size glass jar nearly filled with gasoline from his closet. He took it down to the third floor and went into room 95, which he knew was unoccupied. He sprinkled the gasoline around the rugs and furnishings and then tipped over a paper filled waste paper basket and lit it with a match, which ignited the gasoline. He then picked up the partially filled glass jar and went back to his room and

The Ahwaga Hotel lobby on a lazy afternoon, c. 1920.
Source: Tioga County Historical Society

nonchalantly undressed and lay down to wait until the alarm was sounded. When he heard the cries of "Fire!" he got up, put on his trousers and hurried to assist the fire fighters, pretending to help extinguish the flames. When he was asked why he did it, he said he had no reason. The police asked him if he understood that he was putting numerous people in jeopardy, but he did not answer. He said he had the gas hidden in his room since the last fire to clean his hands from working with tar on the new roof.

Hickein had been in trouble with the law before. He was a married man with three children, but was separated from his wife who was living in Oneonta, and he had been in Children's court for the support of his children. About a year before, he was sentenced to the county jail for thirty days for contempt of court in failing to abide by the edict of the court. It was also found that at one time while employed as a carpenter on the D & H Railroad in Oneonta, he sustained a severe fall from a high scaffold and suffered a fracture at the base of the skull. The authorities believed that he suffered permanent injuries as a result of the accident, which could explain his motive for setting fires. District Attorney George Andrews asked Judge Nathan Turk to appoint a commission to examine him for his sanity. He couldn't believe anyone in his right mind could commit such a crime. Throughout

*A billboard for the Ahwaga that once appeared just outside of Owego.
It was painted by local artist Robert Lee.*

1908 Firemen's parade showing Defiance#5.
Source: Tioga County Historical Society

Hickein's hearing, he acted disinterested in what was being said. He was put in jail without bail and was charged with first degree arson by District Attorney Andrews. The papers noted that he was a model prisoner. The grand jury trial was held in October with Judge Nathan Turk presiding. In part, he said, "Your acts not only endangered the lives of all these people in the hotel at the time, but it has made people fear to stay at this hotel. They have become apprehensive that something dreadful might take place while they slept. I have talked to you before and I believe that you are responsible for your acts. The act of setting fire at night to a building in which there are people is one of the most serious of all felonies. But I am not going to impose the extreme penalty. I could send you to prison for from 20 to 40 years. I am going to give you a sentence, however, that will keep you confined for a considerable time. And people will have the opportunity to get over this fear that they are not safe in their beds. Judge Turk then imposed a sentence of 7 to 15 years in Auburn State Prison.

As an aside, not only was room 95 the site for two fires, but most interestingly, it was the same room where Lottie Richardson and her lover met for their rendezvous in the 1870s. Also, both of the men were sentenced to Auburn State Prison. It seems that the heat was on in room 95, first from passion and second, from arson. Could it have been haunted?

Chapter 6

Youthful Memories

A few of Fran Clark's memories of the Ahwaga Hotel included the time when he was a young man in the 1930s. His family roots run deep in Tioga County. His great-grandfather was Frank Sporer, of the old North Avenue piano firm, Sporer-Carlson-Berry. Fran recalled a time when John D. Rockefeller was staying at the hotel. He walked up near the corner of Ross Street to visit his long time friend, Mrs. Susan J. Life, who lived at 363 Front Street. Fran lived just around the corner on Ross Street and his mother told him to go outside and see him. When Rockefeller spotted Fran he motioned him to come over and said, "Young man, hold out your hand." He put a shiny dime in it and said, "I want you to save this and you will have a good life." Fran thanked him, jumped on his bike and went to the drug store for a "Boy Scout Sundae." Fran said, "It was only a dime."

His family was close friends with Cubby Decker; in fact, he called her "Aunt Cubby." One time she offered him a penny for every fly he caught. When she realized he was catching more than she saw flying around, she found him lifting a few that were already stuck to the fly paper.

He worked as a bellhop when he was twelve for a while and most of the tips he received from the guests averaged about a dime or a quarter; but he remembered a few of them who rented a room during Prohibition for a secluded rendezvous and as Fran put it, "They brought their own booze." They would call him to run down for ice cubes or ginger ale and when he got back they were in such a hurry to get rid of him they often gave him as much as a fifty-cent tip. Sometimes he and a friend would go up on the roof and try to look in the windows of their rooms.

After Prohibition ended and the bar re-opened, he worked in the kitchen washing glasses. Sometimes the senior boys from his class would ask him to get them drinks, so he saved all of the leftover drinks, mixed them together in a big bowl and took it to them when he got off from work.

When he was eighteen, a band was hired to play at the Ahwaga that had a married female drummer. They liked each other and went out on a date, but when his mother found out she gave the drummer a good ear-full about messing around with her son and that was the end of that.

Fran recalled being there on a July morning when Dwight came down the stairs and saw a Ford convertible parked right in the middle of the lobby. He said, brusquely, "What the hell is that doing here?" When the desk clerk, Charlie Dingman, told him it was a birthday present from his father, he was all smiles.

By 1932, Decker decided to raze the old Hiawatha House hotel on Hiawatha Island because it was so dilapidated. He was concerned that someone might fall through the floor or porch and be badly injured. It hadn't been used as living quarters for a long time and over the years, boards from the Hiawatha House were removed to repair the barns on the island, making it a leaky, decayed old relic. He had already moved the beautiful high-backed chairs, mirrors, dishes, pictures and anything else of value to the Ahwaga Hotel in Owego.

Although Tioga County voted to ban liquor licenses in February 1918, the official Prohibition Amendment to the Constitution was ratified January 16, 1919 and went into effect on January 17, 1920. It ended on midnight December 5, 1933. Soon after, the newspapers noted that only four out of the nine establishments that applied for liquor licenses were approved, and the Ahwaga Hotel was one of them. By the following week an ad was placed that read, "Tap Room with Patty Cusick, everything from chowder to champagne. Open day and night." Needless to say, business picked up.

In an interview with Dan Devine, a long time businessman who operated Dip's Tavern out on Route 38, he related how he, too, used to bellhop at the Ahwaga in the 1930s. One of his most memorable recollections was meeting George Bernard Shaw who walked from Dansville and stayed overnight and gave Dan his autograph. He was awarded the 1930 Nobel Prize in literature. Shaw was seventy-eight at the time and an avid health enthusiast as well as a vegetarian. One of his quotes was, "I did not become a vegetarian for my health; I did it for the health of the chickens."

Herbert H. Lehman 1878-1963. The 45th Governor of New York State.
Visited the Ahwaga on October 27, 1952.

George Bernard Shaw 1856-1950. Awarded the Nobel Prize for literature in 1925.
Visited the Ahwaga, c. 1930's.

The week of March 16th, 1936 turned out to have the biggest flood since 1865, which also happened in March when the Susquehanna River crested at 21 ½ feet. This one crested at 22 ½ feet. Water came into the cellars of the stores on Front Street and when it reached the north side, it came in between the Ahwaga Hotel and the First National Bank. The water reached a depth of sixteen inches in the hotel cellar and two feet in the bank basement. They started to pump water out of the hotel at three o'clock in the morning, but it rose high enough to extinguish the fires in the furnaces. There was no heat for about five hours, and using two pumps, they continued pumping for two days. The oil burning furnace at the bank was out and the Owego National Bank on Main Street had four feet of water. Although there was no merchandise damaged, about sixteen inches came into the basement of the Cooper store at the northwest corner of Front and Lake Streets, where Riverow Bookshop is today. The Hubert Cooper family, who had to be rescued from their Armstrong Place home, took refuge on the second floor of the store.

It wasn't long before the hotel was back in shape because at 7:30 P.M. on May 21, 1936, the First National Bank celebrated its 100th anniversary there. An elaborate dinner-reception was held for five hundred shareholders and guests. The newspaper gave all of the details of the bank's history, starting with Gurdon Hewitt, the first president in 1836. Then, Jonathan Platt, William Pumpelly and the Trumans beginning in 1856: Lyman P., George, William S., Frank S. and the current president in 1936, William C. Truman.

Chapter 7

A Cast of Characters

Two of the people who worked there in the early 1940s were Bob and Juanita Sherwood. Bob was one of the bartenders and Juanita was a waitress. The waitresses wore neat white uniforms with aprons. She worked the breakfast and supper shifts for $5.00 a week and tips. The police force was small, so it was not uncommon for the bartenders to personally have to take care of troublemakers. Bob never forgot the night when two tipsy men came in through the Front Street door. One was 6'4" tall and the other was shorter. As they walked past the orchestra instruments, one of them kicked the fiddle so hard it flew up against the bar. When he asked Bob for rum, he refused to give it to him and told him he'd better make good for the fiddle. He replied, "I've kicked better fiddles in my life" and Bob just about flew over the bar and shoved him outside. Over time, Bob sported a black eye or two, and that's probably why his nickname was Slug. He said weekends were rough, because most of the troublemakers came from out of town. A band from Binghamton would play on Friday and Saturday nights for dancing. Their music was the big band style and the tables would be arranged in a circle in the large dining room, with the dance floor in the middle.

A whole cast of characters patronized the place. One man who liked his liquor more than his gun brought a single-barrel shotgun in and traded it to Bob for $3.00, saying he would buy it back, but never did. Another man would come in to the bar quite regularly with a four-quart pail and have it filled with beer "to go." Attorney, Benjamin Loring always came in through the kitchen door. He had a mustache, wore a rumpled felt hat and didn't smile much. Another regular customer was George F. Johnson. Juanita Sherwood remembered that he came for dinner at least once a week with

Robert (Bob) Sherwood, the bartender nicknamed "slug" for good reason.
Source: William Sherwood

Juanita Sherwood, Robert's wife and also waitress at the Ahwaga.
Source: William Sherwood

his nurses and would always order a drink called a "Pink Lady." Since one of the ingredients was cream, he would always insist that Juanita make a special trip to the store to make sure that it was fresh.

For a while the Ahwaga was the headquarters for the Buck Jones Bar-O-Corral which met there for business as well as pleasure. It was a group of men and women who were interested in horses and riding. They performed at rodeos at the Rudin farm on Gaskill Road, drawing in hundreds of people every week in the summer. Most of the profits were given to local charities. It was mentioned that one of them once rode his horse right into the barroom. The entrance to the bar was on the Church Street side of the building and the hotel garage was in the back. It wasn't unusual to see their horses tethered outside of the door.

Definitely, one of the most colorful characters was Susie Ford, sometimes nicknamed, "Tin Lizzie." She lived at Water Street in the village with her stepson and found odd jobs to make a living. One of her oddest jobs was pulling a wagon through the streets, picking up rags and junk to sell to a dealer who probably paid her a pittance. Cubby hired her to wash dishes; and because Susie wasn't too careful with her personal hygiene, Cubby tactfully gave her an old-fashioned long-sleeved bathing suit, hoping that she would go swimming and wash some of the grime away. However, Susie took it and said, "Thanks for the pajamas." Her idea of dressing for work was to wear an old evening gown, covered with a burlap bag for an apron. She caused some people to do a double-take when she went to the bank and would suddenly and unabashedly flip her skirt way up to reach for something in her pants-pocket. Cubby decided it might be best if she hired her to work on Hiawatha Island to do farm chores and that seemed to be the best decision.

The Ahwaga was definitely the place to go, especially for the younger crowd on Friday and Saturday nights. The tables in the dining room would be moved back and a band would provide the music for jitterbugging, fox trots and slow, romantic tunes, a far cry from the quadrilles and waltzes that were the rage in the 1800s. Phyllis Ketchum Watson told me that the hotel was where she met her husband, Eugene Watson on a quiet Sunday evening. She and a few girlfriends stopped in just to chat and play the jukebox. When Phyllis went into the bar area to put some money in the jukebox she noticed

Susie Ford, dishwasher "extraordinaire."
Source: William Sherwood

Lucille "Cubby" Decker, everybody's friend.
Source: Jeanette Baldwin

three sailors sitting there – but not for long. They came into the lounge and after more nickels went into the jukebox, they had fun dancing. Eugene was one of the sailors and danced with Phyllis. Her high heels made her a bit taller than he was, so she kicked them off and had a good time. After he walked her home, she figured she'd never see him again, because he was stationed at the Sampson Naval Hospital, sixty-five miles away, but she was wrong. He came back the following week and it wasn't long before they were boyfriend and girlfriend. He would hitch-hike three or four days a week to see her. Her mother said, "You better marry him before he gets all worn out!" And so they were, four months later. One of the sailors was supposed to be the best man, but didn't show up at the church. While the reception was in progress at her house, the door opened and his sailor buddies came staggering in drunk and noisy from celebrating ahead and were promptly ushered out. The marriage was a good one that lasted fifty eight years before Eugene passed away.

Eudora Shuler recalled the fun she and her husband, Freddie used to have at the Ahwaga at the "Tilly & Billy" parties. Tilly and Billy were a married couple who entertained at the Schnitzlebank Restaurant in Binghamton on a regular basis; but about once a month they would play at the Ahwaga. Eudora said a crowd of about twenty-five people looked forward to the music, dancing and laughter that went on almost all night.

Jane Worthing and Beverly DeWitt remembered how they would always stop in after the movies at the Tioga Theater. After Bev had a terrible accident when she cut her foot on a mowing machine, a number of her friends came to visit early in the evening. It happened to be May 8, 1945 and while they were there, they heard the good news that the war was over (V.E. Day). In a flash, everyone was gone, headed for the Ahwaga to celebrate. Bev was left alone with her aunt, unable to walk without crutches when another friend came by. He had been a prisoner of war and just returned home. He helped her to his car and headed for the Ahwaga. He carried her in and she was able to join the rest of her friends and to feel the warm camaraderie of happiness and relief. The next day a big impromptu parade was held and rejoicing went on for days.

The hotel wasn't through with fires, because in April 1944, another one took place, but this time the damage amounted to only $50. It happened at three o'clock in the morning in the tap room when the coin box for the juke box overheated and burst into flames. Dwight and Cubby Decker grabbed a garden hose, hooked it to a water tap and tried to put the fire out, but the hose was so old, all it did was squirt water all over them and one of the guests that tried to help. However, the firemen were ready, as usual, and extinguished the flames.

The Ahwaga Tap Room was located just outside of the bar in the northeast corner, with folding doors opening into the dining room. Mr. and Mrs. Ralph E. Berry successfully ran the tap-room and made it into one of the most popular meeting places for socializing. It was open every day from eight in the morning until one o'clock the following morning. After 9 P.M. it was open for dancing to a juke box and on weekends it featured live bands. The members of one of them were Gene Kemp, Dan Thompson, Bud Lee, Bill Ballard, John Baron and Bob Franz. The band was known as *Bob Franz and his Knights of Rhythm*. It was the "in" place to go. After the Berry's left, Bob and Madeline Alger managed the tap-room in the 1950s.

It was June 9, 1946 and Dwight D. Decker drowned. He often swam back and forth to the island, but this day the water was choppy and cold. About four o'clock in the afternoon, he jumped in and swam with steady strokes through a brisk current, but it was too much for him. He was carried downstream and when he was just twenty or thirty feet from shore he slipped under the water. His body wasn't retrieved until nine o'clock that night. Cubby watched it all from the shore. She eventually remarried a man named Robert Guess, but it was brief and it ended in divorce.

She continued running the hotel and handling the operations on the island for a couple of years; but closed the island after the river rose to a high level and supplies couldn't be brought over to feed the animals. She had to hire an airplane to drop hay to the fields below while Susie Ford was living alone there working as the caretaker. It was dangerous and a lot of responsibility. Finally, she sold the island to Dr. Tracy Gillette, an Owego doctor, and Susie went back to doing odd jobs around town. Susie died at the age of 82 on November 12, 1972.

Ralph Berry continued on as the manager of the tap room. There were several boarders at the hotel and one of them was John Alden Loring, better known as "Tod," the naturalist who was chosen to go to Africa with Teddy

J. Alden "Tod" Loring 1871-1947. Owego naturalist who
accompanied Teddy Roosevelt to Africa in 1909.
Source: Tioga County Historical Society

Roosevelt in 1909. One evening while he was having his dinner, a salesman joined him at his table and they chatted amicably with each other. After the salesman finished, he went out to the bar where he met another salesman who just came in. Pointing at Loring, he said, See that guy over there? He thinks he went to Africa with President Roosevelt. They laughed and the first salesman told him to go on over and find out for himself. While the second salesman was sitting there listening to Loring tell him stories about Africa, he looked over his shoulder at the salesman at the bar and made a circular motion with his finger by the side of his head as if to say, "He's crazy!" On May 8, 1947 while Loring was having his breakfast in the dining room, he suddenly slumped down and fell from his chair to the floor and succumbed to a heart attack. He was 76 years old. The community mourned his passing, because he was definitely one of the most interesting and intelligent people they had ever known. His father, Benjamin W. Loring served in the U. S. Navy during the Civil War, serving four years, first as acting master, then as lieutenant. While stationed in the Washington Navy Yard in 1865, Lieutenant Loring attended Ford's Theater the same night President Lincoln was shot. He was one of the first to reach the President's box and used his penknife to cut his tie loose and assisted three others in carrying Lincoln to a house across the street. In the process, some of Lincoln's blood got on the jacket of his uniform. The jacket is currently at the Tioga County Historical Society Museum and has been tested for DNA, but because it is so old, the results were inconclusive. Perhaps in the future, testing will be more refined and it will finally be proven.

The winter of 1948 was one of the coldest and because fuel oil was scarce and expensive, Cubby had the furnace converted to coal. Even so, it was a struggle to keep the guest rooms warm enough. Practically all of them were occupied, including some by elderly people who made their home there.

Another important person who came to the Ahwaga Hotel was U. S. Senator John Foster Dulles on September 20, 1949. He had been appointed by Thomas Dewey as a Republican from New York to the U. S. Senate on July 7, 1949 to fill the vacancy caused by the resignation of Democrat, Robert F. Wagner. He was at the hotel campaigning for a permanent seat and was running against Herbert Lehman. However, he lost the election and held the appointed seat only three months, until November 8, 1949. He was later appointed Secretary of State by President Dwight D. Eisenhower and served from January 26, 1953 through April 22, 1959.

Chapter 8

Gone but Not Forgotten

The Defiance Number 5 fire department attracted a lot of attention in April 1950 when they tested their new aerial ladder on the hotel. They probably wanted to make sure it reached the roof after all the times they were called there to put the fires out. A crowd of spectators gathered to watch what the newspapers referred to as "aerial performers."

Louise Woodburn also recalled visiting the Ahwaga. She was impressed by the beautiful wide staircase that led upstairs from the lobby. She and her husband Bob enjoyed having dinner there with their two sons, Robert and David. Years later, Robert was elected the Tioga County Clerk.

In 1954 the Women's Republican Club held a re-enactment of the Thomas C. Platt Buckwheat Breakfast on its fiftieth anniversary and invited his grandson, Senator Livingston Platt as their honored guest speaker. Although the number of participants didn't come close to the number that attended in 1904, the menu was pretty closely duplicated, except they did not serve a two hundred pound pumpkin pie.

The Lions Club used to meet at the Ahwaga in the 1950s and at one of their special meetings they featured Nancy Thomas, a gorgeous blond night club singer from Chicago. She was fairly new to Owego and had a great voice. She had a lucrative career that included singing with Ralph Marterie and his band, on Dick Van Dyke's TV Variety show and in numerous night clubs around the country. While in Atlanta, she met and fell madly in love with her future husband, Ben Phillips. He had accepted a position with a Cadillac agency in this area and they relocated here. After she first arrived, she stayed at the hotel about a week. In fact, she and Ben held their wedding reception there in 1954. One of the waitresses was Anne Boland. Nancy recalled that Anne always wore bright colors with a pretty, little round apron

The Woodburn family having dinner at the Ahwaga. Louise and her husband, Robert, tend to their sons David and Robert. In foreground is Robert (Bob) and David is in the high chair. Bob is the current Tioga County Clerk. Source: Louise Woodburn

tied around her waist. She also remembered a group of murals and pictures of Native Americans that were in the large dining room, along with a huge depiction of Hiawatha Island that originally hung in the Hiawatha House hotel on the island in its heyday. Nancy recalled a very funny story about her teeth. Although she has a perfectly nice smile, she used to use what she referred to as "push-ups," a sort of retainer that slipped over her front teeth to make her natural teeth appear perfectly even. While using the sink one night, she removed the push-ups and they fell down the drain. She begged, cajoled and even flirted with George Dranachek, her friend and manager of the hotel to get them out for her. After using a lot of elbow grease and a wrench, he finally got the pipe under the sink apart and rescued them. It caused a lot of laughs and still does to this day.

Cubby must have been planning on selling the hotel, because by September 1955 she had the somewhat dilapidated second deck of the front portico removed. It was the deck from which Teddy Roosevelt gave his speech in 1910. Fresh paint and other repairs were also completed to make it more presentable.

A collage of Nancy Thomas Phillips' singing career during the big band era.
Source: Nancy Thomas Phillips

1955, Pillars are stacked up after the balconies were removed.
Source: Tom McEnteer collection

Although the balconies have been removed, the building still shows signs of their remains.
Source: Tom McEnteer collection

William Averall Harriman 1891-1986, 48th Governor of New York State.
Visited the Ahwaga in October, 1955.

The very next month, Governor Averell Harriman stopped by on a tour of the state and spoke to a gathering of about 150 people over a public address system in front of the hotel and was introduced by Owego Democratic chairman, David J. Reilhan. At that time, the public works department wanted to widen Front Street and eliminate the broken-arm curve at the east end of Front Street. They claimed it was necessary to remove nearly all of the trees and it caused a public outcry. The governor said, "I can assure the people of this village that as long as I am governor of this state, I will do everything in my power to see that the street is preserved as it is now. Front Street in Owego is one of the treasures of our state." He kept his word, because the trees stayed.

In the meantime, since 1931, the old Ahwaga Hall located next door had been converted into apartments and was owned by Mr. and Mrs. Albert Hubbard. Since then, it was known as the Hubbard Block. In the spring of

1956, Hubbard sold it to George Dranachek, of Binghamton. At the same time, Dranachek also purchased the Ahwaga Hotel from Cubby Decker. She probably felt relieved to be free of it. She used to drive around town with a mannequin next to her on the passenger side of her car and she also placed it near a window in her home to give the impression that she was not alone. But that was hardly necessary, because she had many friends to keep her company.

Dranachek made several alterations to the hotel and kept it open until September 1958 when he sold it to the First City Bank of Binghamton for approximately $122,000, which included the Hubbard Block. John H. Duane, branch manager and vice-president of the bank said, "There are no immediate plans for the buildings; the bank purchased the properties with an eye to future needs. There are no plans to demolish the buildings." But, by the following April, notices were distributed to the residents of the hotel, the apartment renters and the businesses located in the stores connected with the buildings, the Owego Water Works office, Ethel K. Beauty Salon and the Ah-Wa-Ga Barber Shop, advising them on short notice that the buildings must be vacated by May 31st. Demolition was scheduled to begin in early June 1959. Plans were to make a parking lot to accommodate the increasing number of bank customers at their Lake and Front Street location, adjacent to the site where the Ahwaga Hotel and Ahwaga Hall once had their heyday. Charles "Charlie" Underwood was the owner of the Ah-Wa-Ga Barber Shop and first moved to the hotel site in 1957. It was located on the main floor of the hotel, to the left of the main lobby from the front door. After receiving the notice to vacate in 1959, he moved to his present location at 177 Front Street and is still in business. Actually, his is the only business left that had any connection with the Ahwaga Hotel.

Ads were placed in the newspapers to announce the sale of everything that was in the hotel: "Wrecking Ah-Wa-Ga Hotel in Owego." Listed were fixtures, equipment, tubs, toilets, kitchen cabinets, sinks, lights, doors, framed windows, fire doors, modern radiators, plumbing, framing lumber and many other items, including art work and even the slate sidewalks. Freddie Shuler purchased some of the sidewalks and installed them in the sunroom of his home across from Hiawatha Island. The large plate glass windows that were installed in 1909 by John F. Ward were purchased and

A photo of Stack's furniture store, now Riverow bookshop, at the corner of Lake and Front Streets. Source: Tioga County Historical Society

Hotel gone.
Source: Tom McEnteer collection

1959, The parking lot is in, waiting for the new bank. Note the beautiful First City bank building that was also demolished. Source: Tom McEnteer collection

Circa, 1960. The new bank is up, along with its parking lot.
Source: Tom McEnteer collection

re-installed at 228 Front Street. The ad was placed by the Pelnik Wrecking Company, Inc. of Utica and Yorkville.

Many people just shook their heads trying to adjust to the fact that the once grand old hotel was gone, but there are still people around who fondly remember the Ahwaga. However, if it wasn't for the historic marker at the corner of Front and Church Streets, most people today wouldn't even know where it was ever located, let alone its history.

Charlie Underwood, a barber for 56 years, is the only surviving business that was once located at the Ahwaga Hotel.

Historic marker at the spot where the grand old Ahwaga Hotel once stood at the corner of Church and Front Streets in Owego.

$\mathcal{S}$ources

Everts & Ensign. *History of Tioga, Chemung, Tompkins and Schuyler Counties, N. Y.*
Philadelphia, Pa. 1879

Gay, W. B. *Historical Gazetteer and Directory of Tioga County, N. Y. 1785 – 1888*
Syracuse, N. Y. Reprinted by the Tioga County Historical Society 1985

Kingman, LeRoy W. *Early Owego*, Printed by the Owego Gazette Office 1907
Reprinted by the Tioga County Historical Society 1987

McEnteer, Thomas. *A Look at Earlier Days*, *Owego, N. Y.*
Owego Bicentennial Commission 1987

McEnteer, Thomas. Editor. *Seasons of Change, an Updated History of Tioga County, N. Y.*
Tioga County Legislature 1990

Sedore, Emma M. *Hiawatha Island, Jewel of the Susquehanna*, 1994
Tioga County Historical Society

Tioga County Historical Society: Books, photo collection, scrapbooks, genealogical records, obituary files and newspaper files: *The American Farmer, Owego Gazette, Owego Times*

Watros, Hilda. *Owego Reflections 1887 – 1987*, Tioga County Historical Society
Heart of the Lakes Publishing, Interlaken, N. Y.

Index